SOMEWHERE BEYOND

A COLLECTION OF POETRIES

KRITIKA

Made with ♥ on the Notion Press Platform
www.notionpress.com

"To my people"

Contents

Contents

Preface

I started writing when I was in high school. Since then I wanted to publish my book, but the fear of failure always pushed me back, this time, I thought I could do it, and finally after months of planning and thinking here it is.

When I first wrote my poetry, it was because my high school friends pushed me, and since then, I never felt the need to look back. Poetry was there when no one else was. Poetically writing my feelings became my escape.

This is my first book, and therefore it is close to my heart. It contains art that is close to me in many forms because it even has some of the very first poems that I wrote.

Acknowledgements

I want to thank my family and friends for being so supportive of the process of this book and for not letting me give up on my dreams and aspirations of being a published writer. I sincerely thank one and all who have helped me in this journey.

I am forever thankful to my mother (Neeti Kansal) and my father (Sandeep Mittal) for always cheering me up whenever I felt like I couldn't do something.

I want to thank my dear friends who sat with me to help me negate this book in the right direction. I hope this book receives love and gives love.

HURT

1. Getaway

My head's bursting with thoughts;
Like my mind wants to fly
for once in my life, I don't want to try,
All I want is to break the chains
wanna be away from all the pain,
I want to run, fly like the wild
because sitting here, thinking
Makes me depress
no feelings I can express.

2. Oh! How I wish it weren't true!

I love you
But oh! how I wish it weren't true!
you played my heart like a pro
broke into pieces like a mirror,
making me so vulnerable
you promised and then said
"promises are meant to be broken."
I love you
But oh! how I wish it weren't true!
you sweet talk
at nights with me, you walk
all those kisses, and I miss you's
were a lie
all I want to do is die
I love you
But oh! how I wish it weren't true!
at night we cried
at times we laughed
did everything together
but then you left
I love you
But oh! how I wish it weren't true!

3. Burning Hearts

My face pressed against my palms;
The heat oozing from my face
slowing life's pace,
The ticking of the clock
hitting my head like a rock
Open books and a pen;
but not having the will to do anything
I am just no more of a king
feeling so lifeless,
I am a mess
I want all of it to stop
Just no more of something or anything
there is a hole consuming me day in and day out.

4. Lost

I am holding on but still giving up,
I don't know, but I am lost,
wondering in the world all alone
broken and shattered, I am
having questions but no answers
I don't know what's up
and what's not?
I smile and talk
I laugh and walk
but still, I am stuck
What is this feeling?
What is this way?
I am chilling with friends.
But all I can see is that everything has dead end.

5. Devil

I loved you with my soul
not realizing you are a piece of coal,
I gave you my love,
You took my light, my shine, my spark
making my life dark,
I am left wondering, here
to me a minute, you don't spare,
You were my hero and not some villain
but maybe being a monster was in your veins,
You left me alone on this lane
I am broken and lost,
maybe for loving a devil, this is the cost.

6. Too Much

I can feel my mind exploding
I can feel all the blood rushing to my mind,
I feel I will drown in this flood
everything I have been feeling is too much,
What is all this rush?
The world around me is crumbling down
everyone only wears a frown,
I can't think straight
can't fight fate,
I am on the edge of giving up
all this sadness envelop
around me, if you see all the sadness
I know nothing about it.

7. Mingled

Love was meant to be simple
several books that I read, words I listened to,
The poetry etched on my soul,
they all said love would flow and
when its the right one, you will know then
Why does my pen bleed red on paper?
Why do the words I wrote once now scream inside me?
Why the walls around me are scratched, and why it hurts?
Why, when he is **the one** still my heart feels empty?

8. Love is a poison

I loved you softly
you held me coldly,
I thought it was just beginning
not knowing it was my end,
I gave you the world
abuses at me, you hurled,
I thought love was warm
but you taught me love, is nothing but poison.

9. What are we?

You said we are friends
I took us as lovers
You held me as I am yours
then why all this chaos?
When you change your mind,
you were so kind.
Now I am not able to understand you.
They ask me about you.
What should I say?
You didn't break up
You just messed it up
Was your love confined to my body only?
Was this your kindness?
Tell me, what are we?
Claiming each other,
Kissing lips, touching bodies
being in each other's arms
Tell me, what are we?

10. Lie

People are filled to the brim with lies
all here are heartless spies,
People are fake to your face
they change you into one of their cases,
People smile and backstab you cruely
making you die surely,
People call you a hypocrite if you say your mind
they can never be kind,
People demand you to stand by their side
pushing you from life's ride,
Even after backstabbing, they blame
to be your friend, they claim,
Tell to all those people fuck it
die in a pit!

11. Pay for deed

You were a dream, but now a
nightmare making me scream,
I thought, like everyone, you are my lighthouse,
but you made my life chaos,
You were meant to be a treasure
for you, I was just a person to talk leisurely,
You tore my heart open, making it bleed
but God will make you pay for your deed!

12. Goodbye

They say the things which end with goodbye are bad!
They don't know about my hurt, my pain
As you left me alone here
without even saying goodbye.
Somedays you call
Somedays, you leave me here waiting
Sometimes you are mushy love
Sometimes I am just a friend
Somedays, I am the only one
and then I am one of those
Somedays, you consider me rose
tell me I am the dose you need
but then another day again, I am just a friend
it is just a trend
you know, Friends with benefits!

13. Hurting

Tears streaming down the face
head pressed against the bench,
Thoughts making a tangled web
breaking the rib cage,
drying the pen's nib,
I am a writer, a misfit
falling slowly but tragically into this pit
I have no answers left
everything is gone which I had kept,
My body is frozen
I am the next to be hanged,
They stabbed me in the back
the loveliness they lack,
I want everything to stop
Cuz I want to live!

LOVE

14. What is Love?

What is Love?
Is it at first sight
when you can see their plight
Is it when your dupatta gets stuck in their watch
or when they are always in your soch
What is love?
Is it when background music plays
or maybe when he runs to the airport to propose
What is love?
Is it when he learns Guitar
or when he comes 7 samundar paar
Is it when he brings gifts
or when at times he forgets dates
What is love?
Is it when he says stay
or when he gives you space
Is it when he calls to say I love you
or when he hangs up before he hears I love you
What is love?

15. Dear Lover

I am chaotic and a mess
I am not anything less,
I annoy and irritate
but deep down I care,
under all this layer
there lies a heart,
my core apart
that loves you so much
the heart that care,
the heart that beats for you
at days I am too much to handle
All you want to do is surrender,
But on those days
I want you to chase,
Chase our love
get us through our darkest days,
Coz I would do the same
When days like this come in your life
I will be your shield,
I promise dear lover to be there
and get through it
to create our own infinity!

16. Breeze

Lonely in the corner I was
It felt like life was on pause,
But then you came
not to tame
but just to love me,
make me wonder about things I couldn't see
You are a blessing
You are my muse
I can't imagine any other way
without you I can't spend my day
I love you way more than my imagination
You are my final destination! <3

17. Love

Love is a four letter word
beautiful and messy at same time
for lovers, it is their favorite crime,
for today's world it is hard to understand it
for them they think its shit,
Timepass they do
how beautiful it is they have no clue,
I am an old school when it comes to love
No timepass I want
No relationship to flaunt,
I don't want something that in future haunts
I want someone who feels at home in my arms.

18. He

He is the sunshine to darkness
He is the path out from mess,
His eyes are like honey in the sun
the one's which demand you to stay not run
His smile is the light
Yes, he is my Mr. Right!

19. She

She has a heart of gold
she is damn bold,
Her thoughts are so pure
to my wounds she is the cure,
her voice soothes me
feelings are grown
and I am fully drown!

20. Little Girl

When I was a little girl
I was told to believe in fairy tales
and that no nightmares exist,
I was taught love and humanity
But when I woke up from the deep slumber;
All I could see were the bad deeds
evil deeds,
they try to tell me, ask me to believe
My prince charming will come to save me,
but then I told them to wait and stop
I don't need a prince; I need no saving
I am a queen, and I have an empire to build.

21. One soul

Living and hurting
Ain't that easy,
Miles apart
lies my heart,
people say it is not going to work
but they don't know
what him and I are mad up of,
we got each other through thick and thin
a love so pure
a love so love;
nobody can stop us
cuz he got me and I got him
till death do us part.

22. Sunshine

Amidst all these duties and responsibilties
he's my carefree nature,
Amidst all this chaos he's my calmness,
in this hip-hop he's my old romantic song,
In this hookup culture he is my long treasured love letter,
he is my sunshine in this darkness.

23. His eyes

They're different from the ones i came across
they connect to mine
every emotion is transparent,
they make me want to write poetry about themselves,
when they look at me
they make me feel beautiful;
I came across many brown eyes
but none as beautiful and charismatic as his.

24. Dear Love

I don't know whose faces are those who haunt you,
But I promise I am going to take care of you like those few,
Every time you feel uneasy, I will hold your hand tight,
Would never let you away from my sight,
I will make you believe in love again,
A love that is without any pain.

25. Destination

Strangers as we were
not aware of each other,
One fine day crossed paths
and our destinies tangled,
Heartbeats were raised
as our hands laced,
Strangers to lovers
laid under the stars,
You healed my scars
bit by bit I fell for you
and so did you,
Two hearts synced in a beat
no lies no cheat,
A story meant for lifetime was created
since ages this moment by both was awited!

26. letting In

Lonely and lost I was
what I thought would be a dream land
seemed like a nightmare,
Then I bumped into you
and you held me tightly
touched my soul
broke the walls I built
and I let you in my heart
not knowing what will be the end?
But here we are
standing together
trying for each other
holding hands
even now
My heart still flutters at your name!

Poetry is what kept me alive

when everything else faded!

To My Readers,

I want to say thank you for the support and love. I want to tell you to pause, slow down, and not rush. Inhale and exhale and notice the rhythm of your body. Listen to your heart pumping blood. Observe and see the people who care about you; notice the smile they have on their faces every time you enter the room. Look at the art you make. Look at all your achievements; no, I am not talking about trophies or anything; I am talking about performing tasks as simple as living and surviving against the odds. You are unique, and that is why you are here. Say to yourself that "I will be okay." Take baby steps towards healing. Don't rush it; it will take time but know it is worth it.

Kritika, born and brought up in Punjab, started her writing journey in high school. She has embraced poetry and started her blog "andshewrites" and an Instagram page. She is a lawyer in the making by profession, but poetry takes over her heart. This book is a step forward for her to fulfill her dreams. When she is not writing, you will find her reading a book and sipping her coffee in some coffee corner of Hyderabad while she tries to complete her law assignment deadlines.

Printed by Libri Plureos GmbH in Hamburg,
Germany

9 798889 519669